NFT IS THE KEY TO THE METAVERSE

START THE JOURNEY TO WEB3 AS A CREATOR
OR A COACH | LEARN METAVERSE, INVESTING
IN VIRTUAL LAND, NFTS, & VIRTUAL REALITY

MONIKA ALI KHAN

CONTENTS

belonging to a third party, then the reader and only the reader shall be responsible and liable for his/her actions should you suffer or incur any harm or loss from the usage of such information.

By reading this, the reader agrees that under no circumstances is the author responsible for any direct or indirect losses incurred due to using this document's information, including not limited to omissions, inaccuracies, or errors. You agree to hold the author harmless from all (including but bot limited to) claims, losses, damages, etc.

BOOK DESCRIPTION

Do you wish to make money with the Metaverse?

Do you want to learn more about the many opportunities it may provide?

Have you heard about NFTs and the Metaverse?

If you don't, you might be missing out on a huge opportunity in your lifetime!

Continue reading...

The Metaverse is an online virtual environment in which users can interact with the computing environment and other users. It isn't just virtual reality games and chat rooms that show how quickly the Metaverse is growing. It's also moving on to things like cryptocurrency and NFTs, among others.

With the help of this practical guide, you'll learn how to take advantage of this new environment and invest wisely.

This Metaverse book contains the following information:

- How to create, buy, and sell NFTs
- Understanding the Metaverse (Augmented and Virtual Reality) in its entirety

- Advantages and qualities of the Metaverse
- Why NFTs are the key to the Metaverse Economy
- Primary ways to invest in the Metaverse
- Marketing in the Metaverse
- The role of Web 3.0 in the Metaverse
- The Metaverse and the future of gaming
- The future of the Metaverse and more...

Don't lose out on the opportunity to arrive ahead of others. It's now up to you to take action!

INTRODUCTION

After Facebook was renamed Meta, there was a fresh buzz around the term "Metaverse," but no one knew what it meant. For many years, people have speculated on how the internet and technology would progress. Web1, Web2, Web3, and so on are frequent terms used to describe distinct stages of the internet's history, and now we're talking about the metaverse. But put the definitions aside for a moment and think about this: Consider building your ideal alter-ego in a virtual setting where you have complete control over all aspects. You can do whatever you want, own whatever you want, and your options are almost limitless.

Such a scenario was frequently depicted in science-fiction films or television programs. However, it may become a reality soon since there is a lot of buzz in the business sector about getting every layer, technology, and protocol ready to build "The Metaverse." Most debates about what the metaverse contains begin to stagnate at this point. We have a hazy picture of what objects exist in what we would term the "metaverse," and we know which corporations are investing in the concept, but we still don't know what it is. Facebook—sorry, Meta, still don't understand it—believes it will contain fictional residences to which you can invite all of your pals to hang around. Microsoft appears to believe that virtual meeting rooms may be used to teach new recruits or converse with faraway coworkers. This book will teach you more about the Metaverse and how it works. But what's the big deal about the Metaverse? And what does it have to do with NFTs, or living on the internet 24 hours a day, seven days a week?

Let's get started since there's a lot to unpack.

1

WHAT IS AN NFT?

To understand Non-Fungible Tokens (abbreviated as NFTs), you must first determine where they exist - in this case, on the blockchain.

To put it another way, a blockchain is a database that is saved on a large number of machines at the same time. All devices used to be connected to centralized nodes (in servers or Internet providers) under the traditional Internet design, but the blockchain operates differently. No central nodes are required; instead, all devices in the system simultaneously store all information broadcast on the blockchain.

Tokens are a form of record entry on the blockchain. The concept of fungibility is a distinguishing attribute of most tokens. One dollar, ruble, or bitcoin can be exchanged for another user's dollar, ruble, or bitcoin, much like money (including cryptocurrency).

However, not all digital materials are interchangeable. An mp3 file containing a Beatles song cannot be replaced with a recording of Eminem's concert, and a painting by Pablo Picasso cannot be substituted for a painting by Claude Monet. As a result, non-fungible tokens were created with the intent of transmitting unique products to the blockchain.

Each NFT is unique and only exists in one copy; it cannot be split, and all information about the creator, buyer, and transactions is safely stored in the blockchain. An NFT can also be thought of as a digital certificate for a specific entity.

The most reputable markets for buying NFTs

You will see that NFT markets are a vital element of the fascinating new trend of NFTs, which you can read more about here. NFT markets have made it simpler and more flexible for people to access NFTs while also addressing long-standing difficulties with income streams for authors. However, the debate on non-financial-transaction markets eventually boils down to one topic. NFT artists and purchasers would undoubtedly seek solutions to the question "what is the greatest NFT marketplace?" to maximize their creations' value. Although these sites and others are home to hundreds of NFT makers and collectors, ensure that the place is correct before purchasing. Some artists have fallen prey to cosplayers who have advertised and marketed their work without their consent. Most importantly, the rapid expansion of various non-financial-transaction (NFT) markets is a significant source of worry. In this situation, a clear sketch of some of the most well-known NFT markets, together with a detailed explanation, may be beneficial.

Here is a list of some of the most well-known NFT markets that may be of use to you as you explore new territory in the NFT world.

OpenSea

According to current industry standards, OpenSea is not

only the most significant NFT marketplace, but it is also the biggest of the NFT markets in the world. It offers a wide range of non-fungible token kinds, including art, virtual worlds, censorship-resistant domain names, souvenirs, sports, and trading cards, among other things. This peer-to-peer marketplace brands itself a provider of "rare digital objects and collectibles." All you have to do is set up an account to explore NFT collections to get started. You may also arrange works by sales volume to find new artists. OpenSea integrates assets with the ERC1155 and ERC721 cryptographic standards are noteworthy. Purchase, sell and discover unique digital assets such as Axies, Decentraland, CryptoKitties (as well as ENS names), and other digital assets using this platform. Over 700 projects of all types, including trading card games, digital art projects, name systems like the Ethereum Name Service (ENS), and collectible games, are shown on OpenSea. The item mining function on OpenSea is also one of the marketplace's most notable features as a non-traditional trading platform. Designers can build their things and establish their NFT collection using the minting tool. Those designing their intelligent contracts for digital collectibles or games will find OpenSea the ideal marketplace for them.

The Nifty Gateway

Nifty Gateway is the most likely candidate to answer the question, "What is the greatest NFT marketplace? "It is without a doubt one of the most reputable high-end NFT markets for dealing in crypto-art works. The collaboration of Nifty Gateway with leading producers, companies, athletes, and artists is beneficial to the company. To be more specific, the cooperation offers crypto art collectors the opportunity to acquire just one-of-a-kind pieces of artwork. On the other hand, it is pretty tough to get approved on the Nifty Gateway when it comes to crypto art markets. As a result, prominent artists, corporations, and celebrity makers can get access to this online platform. Three main auction methods are

Nifty Gateway also provides royalties since artists may choose the proportion of secondary sales. As a leading non-financial transaction platform, it accepts debit cards, credit cards, and ether (ETH) payments.

SuperRare

The NFT marketplace SuperRare is yet another intriguing NFT marketplace that comes to mind while thinking about the most acceptable alternatives. The website is primarily focused on functioning as a market-place where users may trade in one-of-a-kind pieces of digital art that have been produced in limited quantities. An artist that is a member of the SuperRare network creates original artwork. The platform tokenizes the painting and makes it available as a crypto asset or collectible, owned and traded like any other asset. Many industry professionals commend SuperRare for introducing a fresh approach to online connection with culture, art, and collecting unlike anything else available. The emergence of a social network during the SuperRare marketplace is the game's most notable aspect. Because digital collectibles are coupled with visible ownership documentation, they may be appropriate for use in a social setting.

SuperRare is appropriate for beginning artists with a natural aptitude for invention and inventiveness. It is compatible with Ether, which is the native coin of the Ethereum blockchain.

Rarible

It's hard to have a discussion about the most popular NFT marketplace without mentioning Rarible. It's a basic and simple NFT platform with little hurdles to entry for artists trying to get their name out there. As a result, newcomers to the world of NFT may find Rarible to be extremely useful. Rarible, like OpenSea, is a democratic, open marketplace where artists and producers can sell and issue NFTs. The platform's RARI tokens allow holders to vote on features such as pricing and community rules. Regardless, the user experience is hampered by a disorganized layout, which contributes to the overall poor impression. Rarible's most exciting feature is that it has its own coin, RARI. RARI is an important tool for rewarding platform users who are actively using the platform. Every sale on the Ethereum blockchain incurs a 2.5 percent transaction fee. Along with RARI and ETH, it accepts a number of cryptocurrencies, including WITH, ATRI, and DAI. Furthermore, Rarible is a solid non-financial-transaction (NFT) marketplace for royalties since artists may pick the percentage of earnings they intend to receive through secondary sales.

Foundation.

Foundation is one of the most significant newcomers to the NFT markets that has garnered headlines in recent weeks and months. It has emerged as the most reliable non-financial transaction platform for many crypto art makers. The ability to create collections curated by community members is a distinguishing feature of the Foundation. Creators and collectors alike may encourage young artists to join the Foundation via a collaborative approach. Here, creators must earn "upvotes" or invite other creators to share their paintings. The community's exclusivity and expense of entry—artists must also acquire "gas" to mint NFTs—means it may feature higher-caliber artwork. Chris Torres, the creator of the Nyan Cat, for example, marketed the NFT on the Foundation platform. It might also mean higher prices, which isn't always a negative thing for collectors and artists hoping to profit if the market for NFTs remains stable or even grows in the future. As a result, after selling their first NFT, creators will have simple access to the "Creator Invites" option. Foundation is a wonderful choice for any artist who wants to make a mark and stand out as a one-of-a-kind masterpiece. It takes Ether payments and promises to release new functionality shortly that will guarantee a 10% royalty on all secondary sales.

Create, Sell, And Buy Nfts

If you want to monetize your digital art, images, films, and other media, you can convert them into NFTs and sell them. Here's how to go about it. With each passing day, the popularity of NFTs grows, and there have been cases where these tokens have been traded for millions of dollars. That isn't always the case, though. It is not required to make millions of dollars every time; but, if you use the appropriate tactics, you may be able to make money. Learn how to sell your photos, music, art, films, and games as NFTs at whatever price you want.

How to Buy NFTs?

Now let's get down to business with some NFT trading. Make your way to the market you'd want to shop at. We're looking at the OpenSea right now. Go to OpenSea and click on "Explore" to get a sense of what's going on. Many digital assets, such as images, movies, and other media, may be found here. While browsing, there's a strong chance you'll find what you're looking for. Let's imagine you're looking for the image Zuzu Meowfluff from CryptoKitties. You'll notice that the price is 0.05 Ether if you look at the pricing. It was claimed to be $8.96 at the time of publication.

To purchase it, simply follow these steps:

1. Select "Buy Now" from the drop-down menu.

2. Choose "Checkout" from the drop-down menu.
3. Select "Submit" from the drop-down menu.

You are responsible for paying the gas fee. This is most likely going to be a one-time fee. The Ethereum network charges $18.18 per gram of gas. In total, $26.68 was spent on the transaction. You have now obtained the Zuzu Meowfluff CryptoKitties NFT. This is the image you'll be selling; it's a good time to practice selling NFTs now.

In recent years, you may have heard a lot about this. After selling an NFT for $69 million, Mike Winkelmann, also known as "Beeple," became the talk of the town. Many people now value various NFT collections, which range from sports trading cards and highlight reels to digital residences, augmented reality footwear, and music, at millions of dollars. All ownership rights are recorded in the Ethereum blockchain network's digital ledger.

NFTs are the new type of digital asset. Bitcoin and other digital currencies are supported by Ethereum networks. The fact that they can't be copied and are one-of-a-kind is a significant aspect. They function as digital assets that are only yours and no one else's. People may have photographs and other copies of the digital asset that you hold NFT for, but they do not have the original. NFTs are enticing because of this feature. There's also the possibility that they'll just happen once in a while. You could always sell one later for a higher price. You'd do it the same way you'd do it with beautiful art. They can be purchased with any type of cash. You can also use your credit card to purchase NBA Top Shot. Other platforms may ask you to purchase with a cryptocurrency. Here's how to make NFTs out of your digital assets. We'll do so with the help of the OpenSea platform. If you're an artist trying to make some money, you'll get a lot out of this.

How to Create and Sell Non-Fungible Tokens

Let's say you have a collection of digital art or a Zuzu Meowfluff that you'd like to offer on the marketplace as an NFT. Here's how to go about it. Make it an NFT first, then put it up for sale. We used Rarible in this example because of its low costs and ease of usage. It also has a link to OpenSea in case someone wants to search it. Open Rarible.com and touch "Create" in the top right corner. Create one or more collectibles; many of them, for example, can be used for a collection of images or cards. Then choose "Choose File," where you can upload a PNG, GIF, MP3, or other file types. You can only upload files up to 30 MB in size. Decide on a price that you want to pay. We'll put this photograph of Porto, Portugal, on the list for 0.5 Ether. It will be comparable to $826.91 after a 2.5% service fee. Now, state the name of your NFT, as well as a brief description of it. Decide on your royalty. You'll be able to collect paid for it on every resell if you set up royalties.

The price that is being used right now is the current sale price. "Connect wallet and create" is the option to choose. Connect the wallet you created before. Select "Meta Mask" from the drop-down menu. Now, you must pay the gas fee for your listing to be processed. It's $75.64, or 0.044091 Ether, right now. To sign the sell order with your digital wallet, click "Start." In the MetaMask pop-up, click "Sign." You have completed the listing of your NFT by completing these steps. If you search "Porto, Portugal" on OpenSea or Rarible, you'll find your listing. All of the deals will be displayed on the sale page. The funds will be paid to your digital wallet if it is sold. This can be used to purchase more NFTs or cash out using a Coinbase app.

How to Create an NFT in 6 Simple Steps

Step 1: Choose the work to tokenize.

The very first step is to choose the artwork. Non-fungible tokens can represent any digital file. An NFT can be made from a work of art, a poem, music, or a film. A media file is defined as anything that can be played as a media file. After all, the purpose of the NFTs is to transform digital works of art into "one-of-a-kind" works of art in an age of endless repetition.

Step 2 — Create an Ethereum wallet

Other wallets can be used to serve as your public address and store your private key, but we usually recommend using a hardware wallet (this could be a Trezor or a Ledger.) For whatever reason, you've decided to get your fill while the crypto sun shines, and you have the artistic ability to do so. The only thing you lack is the crypto knowledge to get your work in front of the people who will pay hundreds of thousands of dollars for a GIF and possibly give you money. You're in luck, because I've simplified the entire process and will have your strange cryptographic art published on the blockchain in no time. If you're new to cryptocurrencies, here's a quick primer on how bitcoin wallets work: They are essentially software or hardware that allows you to manage a public address on the blockchain of your cryptocurrency. Even if the owner is anonymous, your cryptocurrency is stored at this public address, which is visible to everyone (unless you do otherwise). Each public address is associated with a private key that can be used to deposit, withdraw, or transmit funds from that address. Consider it a mailbox: anyone can see it, locate it, and mail can be delivered to it. The contents of the mailbox are only accessible to the person who has the mailbox key.

There are two types of wallets: Hot Wallets, which are connected to the Internet and provide greater convenience at the expense of security, and Cold Wallets, which store your information offline and are less convenient for frequent use but provide significantly greater security.

MyEtherWallet is a good example of a hot wallet, whereas Trezor and Ledger hardware wallets are good examples of cold wallets. Yes, you can create a cold wallet with pen and paper, but you'll have to figure out your public addresses, which can be difficult. For users who are new to cryptocurrencies and simply want to sell their work, we recommend MyEtherWallet or MetaMask, and any of the Trezor / Ledger hardware wallets for those who are interested in cryptocurrency storying in general (as well as those who have created a significant value sale and want to keep their earnings safe!). Foundation only provides access to MetaMask.

Step 3 — Purchase some ether

After you've chosen your file, you'll need to buy some Ether. NFT can be done on a variety of blockchains, but for the sake of simplicity, we'll stick to Ethereum. It is the most popular network, and it is supported by the vast majority of the major NFT marketplaces. It is possible that the cost of minting this type of token will be high. As a result, you'll need an Ethereum wallet with at least some Ether in it (the cryptocurrency based on Ethereum). "MetaMask" is one of the simplest to use. It is a free app for iPhone and Android smartphones. The cost of manufacturing NFT is highly variable. It's a good idea to keep at least $100 in Ether on hand, with the understanding that the minting process could cost much more depending on the daily operating price. The process is free on OpenSea, one of the largest marketplaces, due to the type of tokens created by the platform during "minting." You must still connect a wallet to create an account.

Step 4 — Select a marketplace

Now that you have everything in order, you must select a marketplace where you can literally (virtually) manufacture and sell your NFT. Some of the most well-known are

Mintable, Rarible, and OpenSea. We'll go with the last option because it's free and has no restrictions on the type of content you can sell. This means you don't have to be an artist to sell on the site. It also implies that the market is teeming with digital garbage that no one wants. Click on the user icon in OpenSea, then on "My Profile." You can choose how to link your ETH wallet on this screen. If you use Meta-Mask, you can connect it to the platform by selecting "Use a different Wallet" and then clicking WalletConnect. The technique is simple to apply. Follow the platform's instructions, and then "sign in" with your MetaMask app to confirm the Wallet Connect transaction.

Step 5 — Upload your artwork

You can create your first NFT after linking your ETH portfolio to OpenSea. By clicking "Create" in the top menu, you can create a new type of collection. Now Fill out all of the required information and save it. You can now begin the process of minting a new NFT. Select New Item, then upload your artwork and fill in the blanks with the required information. When you're ready, press the Create button. Congratulations on creating a non-fungible token! To sell it on OpenSea, however, you must first access the item you just created in your collection and select the sell option. On the next screen, you can choose which Ethereum tokens you want to accept as payment, whether you want to sell at a fixed price or through an auction, and what percentage of royalties you want to receive from the first and subsequent sales.

Step 6 — Pay the transaction fee

After you've locked and loaded your NFT graphic, all you have to do is pull the gas trigger and watch as your work is uploaded to the blockchain and becomes a unique entity on the network, immutable and unaffected by server failure. The transaction fee ensures that your NFT is mined by whichever Ethereum miner withdraws the contract, thereby pocketing your commission. After that, your newly minted NFT should be available and on the market in a matter of minutes, ready to make the day of the savvy patron who sees it first!

Profitability

So you have successfully made an NFT and posted it on the OpenSea marketplace. So, what's next? Waiting for someone to notice your valuable token won't get you very far. You'll need to promote yourself and make the item appealing to buyers, which you can do by reaching out to an existing community of people who are interested in your work. This is the most difficult component to master because it has nothing to do with the creative process. Yes, it is as competitive and discriminating as the traditional art world. Unless you're a meme or another internet phenomenon, of course. In that case, congratulations: you have most likely discovered a way to profit handsomely from that dreadful photograph that many people have used to mock you.

To Buy NFTs, a Digital Wallet Must Be Created

Before you begin, you must first fund your digital wallet. You must first add money before you can use it on the platform. You must purchase one of these because OpenSea requires it. Ether is a type of digital currency. Consider the entire process to be comparable to that of an arcade, where you must purchase tokens to play the games. Similarly, you must purchase tokens from OpenSea; in this case, the tokens are known as "Ether." Don't go crazy with your ether purchases; instead, start with a tiny quantity.

Let's return to the topic of digital wallets. OpenSea recommends using MetaMask, a Chrome browser plugin. MetaMask is compatible with a variety of digital wallets. OpenSea's plugin installation takes roughly 30 seconds.

Make a password for yourself. On the top right corner of the website, click the icon for a profile. Select "Get MetaMask" from the drop-down menu. Then, for Chrome or any other browser, select "Install MetaMask." It would install a Chrome extension. Select "Get Started" from the drop-down menu. Select "Create Wallet" now. To provide comments, choose "No thanks." Select a password. Make sure you don't forget your secret phrase.

Make a record note of it and keep it somewhere secure. This gives you access to your account as a backup. Approve the secret phrase by clicking "Next." Now select "Next" to link your OpenSea account to the newly formed MetaMask digital wallet. Click "Connect" one more. Your digital wallet is now connected to the OpenSea. You're ready to begin once you've purchased some ether.

How Do You Go about Finding Buyers?

There are 2 ways to sell NFT. Trading an NFT that has previously been purchased. You can sell one that you produced and then put it on a blockchain. You are responsible for paying the charge for minting a token. You must pay the fee associated with it to sell it. The marketplace will decide on the gas expenses, as well as the final selling service fees. What is the best and easiest way to sell an NFT that you have purchased? When you buy this type of token, you are purchasing the right to own it. That NFT can be resold just like any other asset you own. To do so, make sure your NFT and crypto wallet is linked to the market you want to sell on. You can sell it for more than you paid for it. The NFT value is not certain and can change in both the long and short run.

How to Sell an NFT You Mined?

You can sell an NFT that you have created on the platform that you are using to trade it. Set the 'Buy Now' price, or share the terms of the auction. That is the price that you have reserved for it. You can set royalties, and then whenever your asset resells, you will receive some incentives. You can buy and sell the NFTs on one website. You can place the item back on the platform that you want and then collect offers. It is a good way to generate revenue because these markets are highly volatile, and the values are always fluctuating. For example, if you purchase an NFT for $100, the value of it could go up to $1,000 within a year.

If you are looking to predict the worth of the NFTs, you can't do so because the market may drop all of a sudden, and you will face a loss. The process of making your own NFTs can be pretty complex. You'll start by producing the art, music, video clip, or file that you wish to sell. You can take inspiration from OpenSea or Rarible. Then you will have to decide the cryptocurrencies that you would want to work with. Most people use Ethereum since it works well with most online markets, but you might prefer a currency with a smaller user base.

You can use the marketplace you're using to upload your NFTs. OpenSea or Mintable are two options. To keep the network running, the gas fee must be paid. When someone resells your NFT on the majority of marketplaces, you have the option of earning royalties. You can also add some new features but leave them turned off. Once you've sold the token, you'll be able to do so. Finally, you must pay an additional price to have it added to the marketplace that you use. People will then be able to place bids on your NFTs and purchase them. They'll be able to resell them, store them privately, or add them to their collections once they've acquired them. NFTs can be purchased with Ethereum.

2

WHAT EXACTLY IS METAVERSE?

The Metaverse is being discussed by everyone, but what does this digital world of the future look like? The Metaverse is the future frontier for online engagement, therefore marketing and communications professionals should pay attention to it. The Metaverse will alter the internet marketing scene in the same way that social media did. While there is no common Metaverse at this moment, firms are positioning themselves to create one.

The Metaverse is not new, but it rose to prominence with the announcement of Facebook, which decided to name the group's holding company (which controls the Facebook, WhatsApp, Instagram, and Oculus platforms) "Meta" to start a project with this name, a project about which little is known yet. A few days later, Microsoft announced that from 2022 it will integrate the Metaverse into the team's platform with a feature called Mash, with which users will be able to create an avatar to participate in business meetings. The idea is the same old thing. On the off chance that you have seen a film like Matrix, you will handily know what it implies: a computer-generated experience space that individuals can enter and access using a contraption or a gadget.

While gaming organizations have taken the primary actions in the Metaverse course, the virtual world anticipated by the tech monsters will be more sweeping and will incorporate everything from the office to amusement. For instance, you can be in Sydney and your family or companions might be in New York and still you could partake in a supper together lounging around a similar table.

It's a fact there are as yet numerous viewpoints to characterize and hindrances to manage like if on the Metaverse you'll feel everything like, all things considered, what might be said about torment? Shouldn't something be said about unofficial laws and security controls? Metaverse might sound and feel like the eventual fate of online media, yet there is a lengthy, difficult experience to make a trip and a general public to persuade to arrive. A partner of mine just composed a blog entry where he uncovered his perspective on whether the metaverse is actually the fate of the web. Trust this makes a difference!

Metaverse is an augmented simulation space in which clients can connect with each other in a PC-created climate. Then again, we can characterize it as where individuals can meet up inside a huge number of 3D encounters to learn, work, play, make, and mingle. Facebook has rebranded itself to "Meta" to be more than an online media organization. They are venturing into the following figuring stage—metaverse. This stage empowers individuals from all circles and areas to interface, drench and team up to share their insight and experience without the impediment of demography or space.

Metaverse is relied upon to help this present reality economy. The stage empowers individuals to assemble, exchange and put resources into items, merchandise, and administrations. It is interoperable and guarantees the makers, manufacturers, and designers know where their business could be going. Metaverse is a hyperconnected computer-generated reality. It very well may be gotten to from various gadgets—from applications on telephones and PCs to vivid virtual and increased reality gadgets. Inside this virtual world, it's feasible to spend time with companions, family, work, and a lot more seriously utilizing computer-generated reality headsets increased reality glasses, portable applications, or different gadgets. The qualification between being disconnected and online will be unimportant or nearly nothing to say.

Metaverse is the following huge wave, and it sounds promising. Multi-dimensional collaboration and vivid computerized content make another web-based stage, and its realization will change all areas of buyers and endeavor conduct. This is a computerized universe wherein your own advanced resources. Your computerized resources are put away in something many refer to as Digital Spatial Storage or DSS. Your metaverse character is put away in your Personal Avatar or PAV. Your PAV is your advanced symbol in the metaverse that you use to address yourself in there. The PAV will be what you resemble in the metaverse.

The Metaverse is simply a virtual universe designed by humans to create a fascinating digital experience where people can interact, transact business, relax and have fun. It allows you to do everything you can in an ordinary world, but it will be done in a virtual world this time. It is the next Internet.

Before now, the world was brought together by the Internet. It broke the boundary limited by geographical location. So, we were able to interact and transact business even though there was no physical presence. In the world of the Metaverse, we would do more than just break geographical boundaries. We can play games together simultaneously, in the exact location of our virtual reality, while we are physically in different locations. We will have meetings in the same conference room, at the same time in our virtual reality, while physically living thousands of miles apart.

If this all-encompassing Metaverse comes to fruition, it is increasingly probable to be driven by blockchain. Non-fungible tokens, or NFTs, have made full ownership of a digital asset conceivable. You may own a digital asset using blockchain technology, and the cryptographic token will verify they are all yours. The support of the users is likewise decentralized and peer-to-peer, rather than being controlled by a centralized authority such as a government or a bank. This is enormous.

People will not only use the new internet as a result of this technology. If NFT technology is integrated with the latest Internet, people will begin to own digital properties. People will acquire and trade unique assets in the Metaverse, with a level of decentralized peer-to-peer ownership that has never been conceivable before. In a word, it's a notion that entails developing digital environments that several individuals may inhabit simultaneously. Metaverse was borne out of emerging development in technological advancement, which was also influenced by the pandemic. It is all about virtual experiences and digital assets.

Indeed, crypto experts claim to be working on making it real. Gamers, on the other hand, may already be living in it. In general, the entire art world is profiting from it. Even web admins and seasoned online users are attempting to salvage it.

A BRIEF HISTORY

We'll follow the metaverse as it progresses from concept to near-reality, from novelty to the heart of humanity, and from atomized societies to limitless canvasses.

The metaverse is currently evolving into a decentralized community of virtual worlds. Non-fungible tokens (NFTs) and cryptocurrencies can be freely transferred between members of the decentralized metaverse, and users have complete control over the building blocks of a frontier that belongs to no one and everyone at the same time. Because of the decentralized metaverse, individuals have more ownership in these alternate universes.

The concept of the metaverse, on the other hand, is not new. The term "metaverse" first appeared in Neal Stephenson's science fiction novel Snow Crash in 1992, and it influenced people such as Jeff Bezos, Sergey Brin, and Mark Zuckerberg in their desire to integrate the virtual and physical worlds. The origins of the metaverse, on the other hand, can be traced back to the early twentieth century. Human avatars in the novel can communicate with one another, transform into super gods, and do anything they couldn't do in real life. Stephenson described Snow Crash as a virtual reality that surpassed the internet.

In this novel, he creates a Metaverse that is more akin to urban neighbourhoods built on a hundred-meter-wide road known as a street. It has a circumference of 65536 kilometres and encircles a black, round planet. He also mentioned the virtual real estate of the global multimedia protocol group. They were part of a group that built and sold computing machinery, and the residences were built on it. Virtual reality gadgets and concepts, as well as a hazy image of the future internet, formed the framework for a World Wide Web that now hosts parallel worlds in which millions of people from all over the world interact, produce, buy and sell assets, work, and learn together.

Historically, commercial entities such as game developers and Internet behemoths dominated the metaverse, resulting in a patchwork of rich but disjointed virtual worlds such as Fortnite, There, and Facebook Horizon. A new type of metaverse is emerging today in response to these corporate players.

The Metaverse can be accessed via personal terminals with high-quality virtual reality displays on members' glasses, or via white and black public terminals in booths. Users will see it from the first-person point of view. People can appear as avatars in the Metaverse in any shape, but they cannot be too tall, so they cannot scale mountains. Walking is the primary mode of transportation, with vehicles such as the monorail running the length of the metaverse streets on occasion.

HOW DOES THE METAVERSE WORK?

The beauty of how the Metaverse works is that what plays out before you completely depend on you. The features you will be exploring will largely depend on what tickles your fancy. It could be a digital salon, meeting, conference, or your favorite hangout. The first step is to join, and you'll be able to experience your desires. The Metaverse will be a community with an economy. You'll own your space, and by using an online Avatar, you will be able to move, speak, interact, and collaborate with others.

Metaverse works in such a way that you'll have access to complete autonomy where you can both own and rent out virtual lands and properties just like you would own and rent out physical lands and properties. Another interesting feature is the creation of arts and buildings, which you could decide to sell to other Metaverse users by using non-fungible tokens (NFTs) or some other measures of value.

Qualities of Metaverse

Some argue that Metaverse is vague, but you'll notice that this concept is already present in some form if you look around. For example, there are PC games that allow individuals to share an online environment at the same time. Such games then go a step further by allowing players to utilize virtual reality headsets. These games will enable you to take on the role of your avatar. The VR perspective, for example, will allow you to put on its garments. A real Metaverse ought to have the following characteristics:

- It must *always* be connected; it has to be operated indefinitely.
- It must be a shared experience; just as it is in the real world, we get to witness events as they unfold. The coronavirus, for example, is currently affecting everyone on the planet. Similarly, we shall see events in this virtual world as a group.
- It must be possible to purchase and sell things to each other in a virtual economy. This might range from products to real estate.
- It has to be possible for people to participate in activities that combine the real and virtual worlds.
- Everything in the shared online environment should operate together correctly. Let's pretend that some video games are a part of this universe. Your Fortnite and Roblox digital characters should use digital stuff from each other's games.

It won't be simple to turn this concept into a reality. We're talking about a space where a variety of platforms will need to function together. Before they can provide us with a free and open Metaverse, we'll need a lot more improvements. Building the globe, larger and more detailed than any digital area, will require many computers to render and store everything within it.

However, attempts to create this type of environment will continue. Maybe one day, the Metaverse won't be so absurd. After all, today's Internet has had its share of problems. Instead of abandoning the world, we might rather utilize all of our resources to better it. As things stand, it is still a hazy, high-concept construct. It's been described as a set of virtual experiences, locales, and products that increased in popularity as the pandemic's online-everything transformation took place. Taken together, these emerging technologies hint at what the Internet might become in the future.

After that, you'll need to permit different platforms to upload their material. Some companies, particularly social networks, are already investigating this possibility. If a social media firm succeeds, it can offer a service unlike any other. This is why Mark Zuckerberg, the CEO of Facebook, stated that he wished for his social network to become a "metaverse corporation" rather than a "mobile internet firm." In August, he released Horizon Workrooms, a new virtual reality program. Users dressed up as 3D characters and entered a virtual conference room wearing VR goggles. It was similar to Zoom.

The Advantages of Metaverse

One of the most exciting ways that businesses are currently making use of metaverse is through virtual showrooms. These give customers an interactive way to experience products without actually having to buy anything, providing a powerful marketing tool for companies. Feedback from testing is almost instant, allowing any problems with a product to be identified and worked on before a product is launched. This can dramatically reduce the risk of a new product failing in the market.

Virtual showrooms are not just restricted to physical products. Many businesses, from travel agencies to accounting firms, have been able to use virtual reality technology for marketing purposes even though their business does not actually involve selling anything. Virtual reality also has the potential to increase productivity as it can allow employees to work from their homes rather than having to commute to an office every day. This allows companies to reduce their impact on the environment while simultaneously increasing profits by cutting down on travel costs. In addition, it can allow employees to live in a more affordable area, while still allowing them to work for a business based elsewhere.

Virtual reality allows businesses to increase revenue streams, too. This is achieved by allowing people who would not normally be able to visit a physical location to experience it virtually through a metaverse. For example, individuals who live some distance away from a business can still visit its virtual showroom and it is also possible for people who may not be able to afford a product to experience a virtual version of it.

There are many advantages of metaverse to business, including increased revenue streams and reduced costs. Virtual reality gives businesses the opportunity to reach more customers innovatively and engagingly, while also saving money and increasing productivity. It is clear that the metaverse is changing the business landscape and is here to stay. Metaverse is a decentralized platform that uses blockchain technology. It allows businesses to use smart contracts and create digital assets. These assets can be used for investment purposes.

Metaverse is ideal for businesses that want to invest in

blockchain projects. The platform offers a variety of features that make it easy to invest in these projects. For example, businesses can use smart contracts to create and manage investment agreements. They can also use digital assets to represent their investment portfolio. Metaverse is also secure and reliable. The platform has been tested extensively and is backed by a strong team of developers. It is also based on the Ethereum blockchain, which has a proven track record.

Overall, Metaverse is a great platform for businesses that want to invest in blockchain projects. It offers a variety of features that make it easy to do so. The platform is also secure and reliable, making it a good choice for businesses of all sizes.

The Metaverse is a new realm that will combine the real and virtual worlds. This has the potential to alter practically every area of our life drastically. For example, in the Metaverse, we can travel, study, work, consume entertainment, shop, and communicate with others. In this new area, friends and families, creators and companies all can accomplish more and experience things we never imagined imaginable. Creators can be at the center of the Metaverse as well. Individuals and corporations may develop various new types of material for themselves and others to explore, including virtual experiences, virtual places, virtual products, and virtual games.

The Metaverse will open up new avenues for earning a living and compensating for a broad and diversified spectrum of previously unrewarded creative activity. This will transform the way people purchase, sell, and do business online. We can now do and experience things that we would not have been able to do or experience otherwise because of the Metaverse. You could, for example, go around the world, stopping at the Netherlands or Venus. To gain a better understanding of other people's viewpoints and experiences, walk a mile in their shoes or look at the world through the eyes of a newborn. A backstage pass to a performance or a behind-the-scenes tour of your favorite institution is also an option. The Metaverse enhances the richness and immersion of experiences. By reducing boundaries, the Metaverse will change the way we interact with others.

Popular Misconceptions About the Metaverse

Users begin to feel nauseous once they are in the Metaverse. Some people think that being inside the virtual world like the Metaverse will make them feel nauseous. This assumption came to be because the Pied Piper CEO, Richard Hendricks, tried a VR prototype and immediately began to vomit (this scene has made most people accept that you may start to feel nauseous once you are in the virtual world). Still, as the show commenced, it was later noticed that using virtual reality can be amazing and fun and won't cause any illness.

THE METAVERSE CAN BECOME ADDICTIVE

There is a misconception that being in the Metaverse can become so addictive that you won't want to be engaged in physical activities. Users impressed by the metaverse environment will find themselves wanting to be in the virtual world all the time. But there is no evidence to prove that virtual world games can be more addictive than other forms of games. Therefore, it is a myth.

The Metaverse Does Not Encourage Physical Activities

Because of the immersive technology, and lots of activities to engage in and explore, it has been concluded that Metaverse will likely discourage physical activities. People will not want to move around in the real world to do anything. They will prefer to sit all day and enjoy themselves in the virtual world. However, this could be partly true, but there are ways to curb this inactivity in the real world. You can schedule time for virtual reality and then get involved with the activities around you in the real world.

The Graphic Won't Be Clear

There is a misconception that the quality of graphics will be blurred giving you a bad experience. Although virtual reality games have different qualities they offer to their users, the Metaverse remains an exception. People still had the mentality of the last century that virtual reality graphics were not as sophisticated as the ones we have now. They were not sophisticated enough to give beautiful imagery. The Metaverse promises to give the users optimum image content.

The Virtual Gear Is Too Heavy

Many people often say that the gear is too weighty and is not comfortable to wear for a long time. Facebook CEO Mark Zuckerberg has created visual headsets and glasses that are not weighty. Users have the choice to get the ones that suit their tastes. So, if you don't want the heavy ones, you can go for the lightweight gear.

Metaverse Is Not for Everybody

This misconception is very common among various kinds of people. Total immersion in the virtual world like Metaverse will always be accepted as an advanced game for its users. Anybody can play in the Metaverse. It is open to everyone and not some specific set of people. If you think you cannot play it, you can play a big role in the Metaverse by investing in it.

The Metaverse Is a Farce

Since Metaverse has been announced as the new internet in few years to come, some people stated that it is a farce and Metaverse is too big to achieve. Although it is a hypothesized world that will take over Facebook, it is likely to come to reality as the major tech powers are making a move to make it come into existence. The biggest technology brands are making so much contribution to it there are massive resources that each company is putting into it. So, the Metaverse is not a farce. It is the new reality coming soonest.

3

HOW AUGMENTED AND VIRTUAL REALITY IN THE METAVERSE WORKS

The metaverse is at the top of the list of the year's most daring new tech concepts. Because it raised more questions than it answered, the idea swiftly acquired supporters and detractors. If you haven't already decided on a side, now is the moment to discover more about the metaverse: is it advanced virtual reality or something altogether different? Is it feasible to picture it without the use of virtual reality or augmented reality? What benefits do you expect to gain as a result of this?

Does the Metaverse Need AR/VR?

Augmented reality (AR), artificial Intelligence (AI) and virtual reality (VR) all play a role in the metaverse concept. It is possible to incorporate virtual objects into the real world using augmented reality technology. Immerse yourself in a 3D virtual world using 3D computer modeling, one of the most fascinating types of graphic designs. If you're not wearing a VR headset or other accessories, experts believe that virtual reality technology will play an important role in the metaverse's new environment.

As an example, the Facebook metaverse is anticipated to be accessible via VR headsets, smart glasses with augmented reality, as well as in limited ways on desktop and mobile apps in the near future.

Project Cambria, a high-end virtual and augmented reality headgear, has previously been disclosed by the business. There are new sensors that enable for eye contact and facial expressions to be reflected in the virtual avatar, Meta claimed. As technology advances, avatars will be able to use body language and human emotions to create a more authentic virtual communication experience.

Statista estimates that the combined AR/VR market will be worth close to $300 billion by 2024, and Morgan Stanley predicts that it will be worth $100 billion by 2030.

Where is the Line Drawn Between VR and the Metaverse?

One of the most difficult aspects of the metaverse to grasp is how it varies from virtual reality as we know it now. According to the metaverse, virtual reality (VR) is just one component of it. Social networking, virtual reality, augmented reality, online gaming and cryptocurrency are all included into the platform. It is possible to achieve actual telepresence with virtual reality, which differs significantly from the video conferencing we are accustomed to.

In the metaverse, we'll be able to consume material in a completely new way, shifting from 2D to 3D. Additionally, the metaverse is projected to alter the way individuals interact with each other by integrating the virtual and real worlds.

In a remote work setting, for example, it can considerably enhance the degree of communication with a virtual team. By using the metaverse, conventional video conferences may be transformed into meetings where participants feel as though they are physically there.

However, despite the fact that there are still many unanswered concerns about the metaverse, we can still think of it as a large-scale and multipurpose system that can only be experienced through virtual and augmented reality (VR/AR). When it comes to virtual reality, the metaverse has been compared to the next generation of the Internet because of its increased user experience.

Use Cases of AR/VR Technologies for the Metaverse

People believe that the metaverse and gaming go hand in hand, although there are a plethora of other applications given the metaverse's developers' overarching objective of revolutionizing how people use the Internet. Since the inception of virtual environments, the video game industry has reaped the most tangible rewards. According to Activision Blizzard, the company behind World of Warcraft, the virtual world has generated more than $8 billion in real money.

Gamers aren't the only ones that are interested in incorporating gaming into their marketing strategies. Blockchain-based decentralized service Decentraland recently sold a digital plot of land for $2.5 million to a Canadian investment firm using non-fungible tokens (NFTs). Virtual reality fashion displays will be held here, as well as the expansion of e-commerce services in collaboration with fashion labels. This is an example of how internet virtual platforms may provide businesses with additional marketing alternatives.

There is a virtual office space that may change with the evolution of metaverse, as we've already discussed here. This technology, as opposed to the more common Zoom and Skype, gives the impression that the entire team is physically there at the same time. The metaverse goes beyond the services listed, which include picture masking, which allows you to alter the background of a meeting while it is still taking place. 3D-rendered avatars based on your actions and even facial expressions can be used to represent you in the virtual conference

On the market, we may already find such applications. A virtual reality and mixed reality service called Virtuworx provides a variety of customized solutions for businesses, virtual meetings, and other events.

The metaverse has the potential to assist a wide range of industries, including advertising, tourism, education, entertainment, retail, design, and engineering, to name just a few. There is always the possibility for a physical action to affect the metaverse.

THE ROLE OF WEB 3.0 IN THE METAVERSE

Of late, I have seen many people use "metaverse" and "web 3" interchangeably. While both point to a better, improved future, these two concepts shouldn't be conflated as they have different meanings.

Web 3.0 is a well-defined and specific paradigm that offers clear solutions and improvements to certain pitfalls of web 2 (the internet as we know it right now). It is a response to the walled-garden ecosystems that companies like Google and Facebook have created, which is leading to non-consented extraction of people's data, privacy breaches, and the inability of content creators to control their content.

Web 3 subverts the current internet model by directly addressing issues relating to ownership and control. By building the internet on the blockchain, data is open and shared, and collectively controlled by peer-to-peer networks.

The consequence of this is that users become the sole owner and controllers of their data, and peer-to-peer transactions no longer need middlemen. Furthermore, data remains available on the blockchain as a public product that anyone can monetize or contribute to.

Web 3 initiatives are already bringing about some incredible new consumer behaviors. For example, creators can sell content as NFTs, play-to-earn games are helping people earn a livelihood, and community-organized investing collectives are mobilizing substantial capital to bid for certain projects.

Although web 3 is clearly a powerful tool that can transform how we manage data and govern and exchange money, the slowness of completing blockchain transactions limits the use cases in which web 3 can be applied.

In short, the idea of a fully decentralized internet might sound enticing, but there is little impracticality to it. So, while we may argue that web 3 is a crucial building block in the development of the metaverse, it's clearly a single component of an even greater sum.

By acknowledging that web 3 is simply a building block for the emerging metaverse, we are opening up opportunities for potential contributors instead of antagonizing them.

You are a content creator, but does the content you post on Facebook and Instagram belong to you or Mark Zuckerberg? I'm sure you also know the correct answer to this question. Well, that is how things used to work, but web 3 is offering us better alternatives to web 2.

First, to understand the role web 3 will play in the metaverse, you must first understand what decentralized web entails. The current web 2 is centralized in the hand of a few big corporations, but we're rapidly evolving into web 3, and that is about to change how things work.

Simultaneously, the metaverse is how the internet will seamlessly integrate with our lives and how our interactions and communications change. Let's explore the differences between the metaverse and web 3 and how they both complement each other.

Web 3 is a concept for the next evolution of the internet.

It involves the evolution from big tech owning and controlling user content to the users being able to own and control their own creations, digital identities, online assets, and digital content.

In web 2, companies are afforded the luxury of developing products and services on a centralized server. For example, Facebook (now Meta) owns all the content you post to Instagram, and they have complete control over them.

Should they want to ban you and forever stop you from accessing your content, they can do just that.

Fortnite is another example of a platform that gives users zero control over in-game assets and identities. Web 2.0 limits users from controlling and monetizing their content. Over 2.5 billion game players across the world believe they own in-game assets, but that's not the reality.

Unless your assets are on a blockchain-based game in the form of NFTs, you don't own whatever you think you do on the game.

On the contrary, web 3 gives you ownership and control over your content, offering you opportunities to monetize them through blockchain tech and cryptocurrencies. Blockchain enables user interactions with digital services governed by peer-to-peer networks, i.e., a decentralized computer network in place of an entity-controlled single server.

This means that instead of creating content for big tech companies to monetize, you can use search engines, social media, and other decentralized apps based on the blockchain because they let you control your data.

Elements of web 3 are already emerging in the cryptocurrency space. This is evident in the rapid development of non-fungible tokens and decentralized web browsers, which let you choose websites that can access your browsing data. These also block ads so you can have an ad-free browsing experience.

We've established that web 3 is primarily about who will "own" and "control" the internet of the future. The metaverse, on the other hand, focuses on how we will experience this internet. This is the defining difference between web 3 and the metaverse.

The moment Facebook announced its vision of the metaverse, there was an internet-wide outcry that Big Tech will once again take over the metaverse and force virtual worlds to operate with a walled ecosystem once again.

What people fail to see is that Meta's innovation focused largely on hardware and input interface, which we frankly don't have yet. Facebook is trying to solve the problem of full immersion, which, you'll agree, is crucial to other overall processes.

Think about the last two years you've spent on Zoom. How worn out have you been? Now imagine how you will feel having to wear a VR headset around all day.

If you are excited about the prospect of spending time in the metaverse enjoyably, you need more natural, expressive, and immersive virtual interfaces. Meta does not in any way undermine decentralization or the work of web 3 with its AR/VR technological developments.

People will begin to construct web 3 applications within emerging 3D forms like AR, VR, and holographic projections, which is the best-case scenario I see.

I also want to talk about the sensationalized option that web 2 will become obsolete after the full-scale implementation of web 3. Again, this is impractical; it is hard to see a world where this happens.

Despite the shortcomings and pitfalls of web 2, there are still products that won't run effectively as designed on the blockchain. Twitch, Discord, etc., are platforms where people can broadcast or communicate in real-time and at scale.

Also, businesses like Uber, Doordash, etc., successfully queue demand to make it match supply. Whether we like it or not, centralization has certain advantages. OpenSea is a centralized marketplace that facilitates and processes transactions on the blockchain. Another good example is Coinbase which enables cryptocurrency transactions.

In these two cases, both marketplaces accept a % as service fees like every other web 2 marketplaces.

While hybrid products don't completely align with the decentralization ideology, they serve as crucial "bridging products" for easier and widespread adoption of web 3 components to appeal to the mainstream. Just as Snap Stories was popular among teens but generally dismissed among older users, Facebook's adoption of stories has made it a mainstream product among all demographics.

It is usually seen as a revolution when new tech and paradigms emerge. But what has happened consistently throughout history is that new tech builds on existing foundations. The email was invented in Web 1.0, but it remains a crucial part of our daily lives today.

All of this is to say that we must focus on the connection between web 3 and the metaverse and how they can complement each other to make better realities available to humanity instead of "choosing aside."

The latest developments in web 3 are a massive leap forward in the journey to building a decentralized internet. However, web 3 is only one component and shouldn't abandon other complementary initiatives.

Both metaverse and web 3 technologies are perfect supporters of each other. Web 3 can serve as the ground for interconnectivity in the metaverse. But then, the metaverse's creator economy can nicely supplement web 3's vision of an entirely new financial world with decentralized solutions to real-world problems.

Web 3 is shaping up nicely with the mainstream growth of NFTs, DAOs, and P2E games. However, we still have a long way to go in the complete development of the virtual world. One thing is certain, though, web 3 metaverse manifests open and decentralized virtual worlds.

I am excited to see how web 3 and the metaverse will shape up over the next few years!

4

NFTS IN METAVERSE

To understand an NFT, it's essential to first learn what is a fungible item. Imagine that you have a ten-dollar bill and I have one as well. You give me your ten-dollar bill and I give you mine. Has the value of your bill or mine changed as a result of the exchange? Absolutely not. The same idea works in the cryptocurrency world. Two people can exchange a bitcoin for a bitcoin without gaining or losing value. This type of item whose value doesn't change after an exchange is called a fungible token.

An NFT is different: It's a unit of data on the blockchain technology that can't be interchangeable. No two NTFs are identical, even if they look the same to the human eye. They're like identical twins who appear similar to the eye but have different fingerprints. Every NFT has a unique digital stamp, making it different from any other NFT. An NFT's digital stamp serves to verify authenticity and ownership, whether the item is digital or physical. Linking of an item to a digital stamp or signature is called tokenizing. Whether you own an animation, a music clip, a concert ticket, or a digitized artwork, you can assign it a digital stamp. In other words, you can turn the item into an NFT. You can do the same with physical items. For example, Nike released an NFT linked to a pair of sneakers called Crypto-kicks in December 2018. When you purchase those sneakers, Nike will give you an NFT to identify you as their buyer and rightful owner.

An NFT is built on a software framework called blockchain, a public digital ledger for recording and tracking transactions in real-time. Any computer with access to the blockchain, called a node, can authenticate a digital asset. This means that there are millions of nodes that can prove a transaction in the blockchain to be genuine. Similarly, some transactions can be deemed inauthentic and be kicked out of the blockchain. Blockchain is designed so that every digital signature or transaction is unique, making it difficult to duplicate digital assets. You can try, but the cost of doing so is high, it won't make sense financially.

The creation of an NFT on the blockchain network is called minting. The majority of minting takes place on the Ethereum blockchain network. To mint an NFT, you first must create a cryptocurrency exchange account from exchanges, such as Kraken, Binance, or Coinbase. A cryptocurrency exchange is a place to buy and sell cryptocurrencies. The reason you open a cryptocurrency account is to buy cryptocurrency to pay the minting fee. In many cases, you'll buy Ethereum, since it's used in many NFT marketplaces.

An NFT has three crucial qualities to serve its purposes: It's indivisible, cannot be destroyed, and is authentic. Cryptocurrencies, such bitcoin, can be subdivided into smaller units. Bitcoin can be split into satoshis, just as the dollar can be subdivided into cents, dimes, and nickels. It's not the case with NFTs because each exists as a whole item. Their authenticity stems from the fact that they cannot be copied or duplicated because they're based on the blockchain technology. Once minted, an NFT exists forever because information stored on the blockchain cannot be erased or destroyed.

NFTs are popularly used to secure content in the digital content industry. This helps content creators deal with privacy and can keep their content safe. Other areas of application include in the gaming industry, memorabilia and collectibles industry, music, and in the metaverse for the creation of distinctive avatars

NFTs as the Key to the Metaverse Economy

Ask anybody about NFTs now, and they would likely tell you that they are mere digital images and artworks selling for ridiculous prices. However, non-fungible tokens have many use cases many people currently remain unfamiliar with. The NFT-Metaverse connection is one of the most promising use cases for NFTs,

The future of NFTs offers investors, hobbyists, and enterprises many fresh opportunities that will shape up its usage and adoption in the new future.

Apart from the fact that they present new investment opportunities for people who are familiar with the blockchain and crypto space, NFTs will be key to accessing the metaverse. Some of the questions I answer here include: Will NFTs be the key to the metaverse? Will they shape how the metaverse will turn out in the future?

Everyone following the blockchain space understands that the NFT-Metaverse interconnectedness is one of the most prominent highlights. Let's talk about how NFTs will play a vital role in the metaverse.

Nearly every discussion around the metaverse suggests that the metaverse and NFTs will blend together to create the new virtual economy we are trying to build. Similarly, some people assume that NFTs are just a smaller component of the broader metaverse. However, you will soon find that NFTs and the metaverse are almost synonymous in nature.

One of the reasons for this assumption is the sudden burst of growth that NFTs have witnessed in the blockchain gaming industry. Obviously, the metaverse can only shape up through virtual worlds – many of which currently exist in the gaming industry. Interoperable games will drive the metaverse's development by serving the online VR worlds.

Additionally, NFTs will open up access to the metaverse with digital avatars associated with real-life identities. In other words, our immutable virtual identity in the metaverse can only be linked to our real-life identities through NFTs.

The earliest example of the NFT metaverse token became evident with the example of NFT-controlled access. In 2019, the very first NFT conference was held; entry to the event was only possible with NFT-based tickers.

Even if no one would call the event "the metaverse" because it is a singular event, it most certainly serves as a clear example of the NFT-metaverse interplay. With this good benchmark, several new projects are being established to take advantage of the interconnection between the metaverse and NFTs.

Most of these projects are focused on massively changing the approach to online interaction. An excellent example is Decentraland, which allows users to purchase ownership of the virtual real estate in the metaverse with associated tokens.

The metaverse is a huge concept, and NFTs will play a crucial role in the broader ecosystem. Metaverse projects would increase the possibilities of NFTs serving as title deeds to virtual properties. They could also require NFTs to gain exclusive access to specific locations in the metaverse, alongside general ones.

I find it particularly intriguing that NFT smart contract functionalities could make it possible to sell real estate in the metaverse. In the early stages of development, NFT use cases in the metaverse would primarily highlight NFT-controlled access.

Similar to the first-ever example of NFT implementation in the metaverse, NFT-controlled access would help ensure VIP access to events in the metaverse or the real world itself. Also, NFTs could play a vital role in airdropping merchandise or special privileges to fans of different brands.

Overall, non-fungible tokens would drive engagement efficiency and introduce interoperability outside the virtual worlds in the metaverse. Evidently, the metaverse and NFTs are two sides of a coin – they are made for each other.

In the quest to understand whether NFTs will be the key to the metaverse, you have discovered the different use cases of NFTs in the metaverse and how they will contribute to its development. Still, it's crucial to identify the significant role NFTs will play in shaping the metaverse's fundamental design.

You have probably observed that NFTs will disrupt the traditional social network precedents of socialization, interaction, and transaction in the metaverse. The question is, how would these effects impact the metaverse in a broader sense?

Here are some of the ways NFTs will impact the metaverse when it becomes fully operable:

- **An open, fair, and transparent economy**

Right now, individuals and businesses could easily

convert real-world assets and services to NFTs in a decentralized digital space. By synchronizing new gaming models with interoperable blockchain gaming, the metaverse can become even more open to physical, real-world assets.

With newer gaming models such as the play-to-earn model, NFTs will assume a more prominent role in the metaverse. This will offer empowerment to players while driving engagement in the virtual world. Plus, play-to-earn games will concede ownership and control of gaming assets to players, thereby fostering a fair and transparent gaming experience.

In play-to-earn gaming, there are guilds – intermediaries – who purchase in-game assets, lands, and other resources to lend out to players who can then use them to earn yields in various virtual worlds. These guilds take a percentage of the earnings in return.

It is impossible to overlook the significance of the gaming guilds in the development of the metaverse economy. The guilds can give a headstart to skilled players with limited or zero upfront capital, thereby lowering the barrier to entry.

This obviously shows the potential for a fair and transparent economy in the metaverse – one where everyone can participate with or without upfront capital. Gamers and other users can also trade their digital assets on NFT marketplaces without restrictions.

It is evident that NFTs are the key to transparency and immutability in the metaverse. In order for us to have an open and fair economy, these properties are highly important. Now, the normal law of supply and demand will drive NFT scarcity, increasing their on-chain value.

Consequentially, there are zero potentials for artificial value inflation. Therefore, you can see how NFTs will help create a fair and transparent economy in the metaverse.

- **New community, identity, and social experiences**

NFTs will also help in transforming the community, social, and identity experiences of participants in the metaverse. For instance, users will be able to show support for a brand or project by holding associated NFT assets.

The result of this is that like-minded NFT holders would form new communities where they can share experiences and collaborate on content creation. One of the obvious examples of how NFTs are transforming the physical world itself is the use of NFT avatars.

Avatars are virtual representations of an individual's actual identity and imagined identity. NFT avatars could serve as access tokens for users to enter and exit different locations within the metaverse. You can think of NFTs as an extension of users' real-life identities, which give complete ownership, control, and flexibility in the creation of virtual identities.

With these avatars, users can gain membership and exclusive access to a wide array of virtual experiences in the metaverse and the physical world. Thus, combining NFTs with metaverse projects offers an opportunity to improve the community and social experiences for users.

NFT avatars are being applied in content creation, and startup launches in the metaverse further highlight their potential.

- **New real estate trends**

Virtual worlds translate to plenty of virtual space, lands, and real estate. NFTs could be used to assume complete ownership of spaces and lands in the metaverse. Thanks to the blockchain, it's pretty easy to prove ownership of NFT assets alongside associated virtual real estate.

A notable use case of metaverse projects like this includes the buying and selling of virtual land for profit. Additionally, you can rend out lands in the metaverse for passive income alongside developing structures such as online malls and shops or event hosting.

Again, Decentraland is the most notable example for highlighting how digital real estate will play out in the metaverse. Recently, Decentraland collaborated with Adidas to host a virtual fashion show.

The exhibition included the auction of various fashion designs in the form of NFTs. So, it's a no-brainer that auctions will take place in virtual spaces in the metaverse. As you will find out, the increasing popularity of virtual real estate has made musical artists more interested in how they can use NFTs to exercise ownership over their art.

Eventually, virtual real estate would broadly refer to digital asset ownership in the near future, and everyone would have an NFT that would give them access to different spaces in the metaverse.

The bottom line is that NFTs have numerous potential use cases that will define the metaverse. While the metaverse will be the digital world where opportunities are limitless, NFs would hold the key to the ownership and uniqueness required to work, live, and operate in this virtual world.

While many continue to assume that NFTs are just a small aspect of the metaverse, and some believe that NFTs will be the foundational blocks to the metaverse – it is obvious that NFTs would open up a wider range of opportunities in this unified virtual world.

NFTs and Virtual Events

NFTs and the metaverse are gaining traction, and they will surely have an impact on every industry in the next years. NFTs might be used to sell event tickets, for example. Consider the following scenario: your organization is hosting a virtual event. Users are sent to a special landing page where they can register for the virtual event by entering their details.

You can send visitors an NFT ticket to the wallet address specified instead of a normal confirmation code through email. This NFT is one-of-a-kind and can't be duplicated. To enter the virtual event, the attendee must have the NFT ticket in his or her wallet. NFTs can be utilized as collectors and even traded or sold by attendees, in addition to enabling safe entry.

The number of events held in metaverse zones such as Decentraland and The Sandbox is anticipated to increase as more corporations and investors purchase land there. From music halls to retail stores to gaming stadiums, landowners have the opportunity to create any type of experience they want. Attendees will be able to view content, play games, network, and even buy goods for their avatars when they arrive at the events.

POAP NFTs

POAP is an acronym for Proof of Attendance Protocol. These NFTs show that you were there at a specific event or participated in a community at a specific time.

While having an NFT that verifies you were somewhere certain at a specific time may seem unusual, it is actually a lot of fun.

The Crypto Punks are perhaps the most well-known

POAPs you've heard of. As of December 2021, the biggest sale was $532 million. (It should be noted that this was most likely a wash-trade; the next highest sale was for $10 million.)

Many crypto and NFT communities are now giving out these digital tokens in order to interact with their members and give them a lot of benefits.

ERC-721 tokens are POAPs. It was originally constructed on the Ethereum mainnet, but in October of last year it was relocated to the Ethereum sidechain xDai. Users can claim tokens from xDai by paying little to no gas fees. Additionally, xDai promises a speedier transaction.

Attendees of both virtual and offline events receive complimentary attendance badges from event organizers. Because each badge is one-of-a-kind, an individual can only receive a POAP if they attend the event. As a result, these tokens prove that the bearer was present at a specific event at a specific time.

Furthermore, because each POAP has a unique design, they make excellent NFT collectibles. The project's creators have also designed an iOS and Android app that allows users to display their prized collections accumulated through visiting crypto events around the world.

Giraffe Tower NFTs

The Giraffe Tower is a 10,000 NFT collection that is part of a wider ambition to bring creators together in the community and help them generate more money than they ever imagined possible. Gary Henderson launched the project in October 2021. The Giraffe Tower collection sold out on 13th March 2022. It is a metaverse for creators that like to make money!

The Giraffe Tower is a realm of grace, beauty, love, and

joy in which family is important and lifelong friendships are established. They stand tall and balanced, their feet firmly planted on the earth, reaching upward and looking ahead. Their necks may soar as high as they need to in order to achieve their objectives and goals. Only 10,000 Giraffes will exist, but beware: they are camouflaged as Aliens, Reptiles, and Zombies, to name a few. You will become a member of the community if you own a giraffe, and you will be able to develop your "Giraffe" family, attend private events, use the learning library, and much more. This isn't just another photo assignment. This is the start of a future ecosystem powered by a one-of-a-kind social utility coin that has never been seen or imagined before. By holding a Giraffe Tower NFT you have access to Virtual Events.

- When you hold 1 giraffe – you have access to the Giraffe Tower
- When you hold 2 giraffes – you can create Baby Giraffes NFT (Giraffe Tower Offspring)
- When you hold 5 giraffes – You can vote in the community
- When you hold 25 giraffes – You gain a Journey role
- When you hold 50+ giraffes – You gain the Whale role
- Every giraffe earns 1 $GLEAF per day
- If you have a hoodie NFT Giraffe you will belong to hoodie gang secret channel on discord
- If you hold a headset NFT giraffe you will have access to a headset channel on discord
- If you have a Giraffe NFT with a Gary trait you may get merchandise such as a Gary Cap

Staking: You can stake your Giraffe NFT and earn 1.5 GLEAF per day per Giraffe.

Breeding: When you have 2 NFT Giraffes you can make Baby Giraffes (Giraffe Tower Offspring).

GLEAF utility token – You earn 1 per day per unstaked Giraffe NFT

To learn more about the collection visit OpenSea websites:

https://opensea.io/collection/giraffe-tower

https://opensea.io/collection/gtoffspring

5

HOW TO INVEST IN THE METAVERSE

The Metaverse has been the most recent investment hype, and here are some ways for investors to gain exposure to it.

Investing in metaverse games like the sandbox (SAND), Axe Infinity (AXS) and Decentraland(MANA), is one of the most straightforward and cost effective way of investing in the Metaverse . To obtain the cryptocurrencies issued by these companies, simply go to a cryptocurrency exchange such as Binance and buy them. Owning a small amount of Ethereum is a low-risk way to gain exposure to the cryptocurrency market (ETH). Furthermore, as the Metaverse and the NFT gain popularity, Ethereum will be more widely used, increasing the cryptocurrency's value.

Non-financial tokens (NFTs) can also be used to invest in these Metaverse games, such as purchasing land in The Sandbox or Decentraland. These NFTs can be purchased via platforms like OpenSea, either through an auction or a "buy it now" option. The disadvantage is that the initial prices of many NFTs are relatively high, which is a significant disadvantage. The cheapest land for The Sandbox currently available for purchase, according to OpenSea, is around $3500.

In addition to digital currencies, a few equities are closely linked to the metaverse, such as Facebook's Metaverse, Roblox's RBLX, and Matterport's (MTTR), each of which has a distinct future promise. Meta, also known as Facebook, is a social networking platform that also owns the virtual reality equipment company Oculus. People can socialize and create on Roblox, a game, but Matterport is a startup that uses cameras and software to digitize the real world so that it can be represented as virtual space, which sets it apart from Roblox.

Investing in the Metaverse ETF (META) is also an easy way to own all metaverse-elated stocks. The Metaverse ETF owns all three of the aforementioned stocks and will regularly update its holdings in response to the company's growth and future prospects over time. Despite the 0.75 percent management fee, the ETF has the potential to save investors a significant amount of time and effort.

Marketing in the Metaverse

Digital marketers must keep up with the most recent technology advancements. Knowing the metaverse and its potential is part of this. Marketers have to realize that the metaverse is not simply a fad; it appears to be here to stay and on its way to becoming the next big thing.

What strategies may marketers use to adapt as the metaverse grows? First and foremost, marketers must remember the importance of millennials and Generation Z as a target market. Certain kinds of metaverses, like games such as Roblox and technologies like virtual reality, are also popular among these generations. Let us look at how advertising can be conducted in the metaverse.

- Parallel metaverse marketing within real-life marketing

Create promotional experiences that are related to or similar to the real-world activities of your company. For the Kentucky Derby, AB InBev's Stella Artois beer brand collaborated with Zed Run to create a Tamagotchi-inspired experience. The main reason for this was that AB InBev's Stella Artois is well-known for its support of sporting events, particularly horse racing. As a result, it appears that developing a virtual platform for NFT horses to be sold, bred, and raced is the next logical step for them

- Immersive experience

You can provide digital marketing in the metaverse space. Bidstack, a game ad tech firm, shifted from physical-world outdoor marketing to virtual billboard marketing.

However, virtual billboards are not the only option. Because metaverses are engaging and interactive by nature, it is ideal to capitalize on this by providing a similar interactive experience with your promotions and marketing efforts. Instead of merely posting commercials, offer branded installations and events that people may engage with.

Early adopters have provided interactive experiences to their customers, such as a Lil Nas X performance in Roblox, Gucci Garden experience visits, and Warner Bros.' 'In the Heights' advertisement featuring a digital replica of the Washington Heights area. Partnerships with the Roblox metaverse and other metaverses have provided businesses with new revenue streams.

- Make collectibles available

Individuals like collectibles, and the metaverse provides them with yet another platform to do so. You may reproduce the experience in the metaverse by providing products or unique items that can only be obtained in the metaverse.

The Collector's Room, for instance, is available in the Gucci Garden Roblox experience. In the metaverse, it enables users to gather limited-edition Gucci products. Gucci made a total of 286,000,000 Robux from the game's early sales of collectible products.

- Engage with existing communities

The public generally dislikes advertising. As businesses aim to break into the metaverse, they mustn't irritate those who are already there. You will also need the favorable feedback of these users because you will be marketing to them.

Note that you may not simply enter a new system without taking into consideration the new layout. For instance, in Roblox, businesses gain more traction when they collaborate with members of the Roblox developer community to create products and experiences. Likewise, when O2 put up a performance on Fortnite, they teamed up with developers who were experts on the game.

Consider this a form of influencer marketing. Community members become key aspects of the implementation of the marketing since user-generated content is vital.

- Continuously experiment

Marketers are living in a fantastic era. While some fundamental principles can aid marketers in determining which approaches and methods to employ, the metaverse is still a young platform with lots of room for experimentation.

Best practices are still being established, and paradigms in their whole are still being developed. This gives marketers a lot of leeway to try new things and come up with unique methods.

6
_____

METAVERSE AND CREATOR
ECONOMY

Many of us are curious about the metaverse's influence on social media. What will it mean for businesses and consumers, and how will it integrate into the emerging creative economy?

The metaverse's objective is to provide a genuinely immersive experience that uses "spaces" to mimic our real lives. These areas will be designed to attract visitors and allow them to interact with AR and VR technologies to do nearly anything. While it may appear to be a novel concept, the metaverse has been present for over two decades, beginning with Second Life and more recently with games like Fortnite.

As the metaverse begins to play a larger role in our lives, we will soon be attending concerts, working out, having meetings and consultations, and socializing there.

Mark Zuckerberg, the founder of the newly renamed Meta, previously known as Facebook, hopes to create 10,000 jobs for the metaverse in Europe alone over the next five years. Virtual reality (VR), blockchain, and non-fungible tokens are just a few of the technologies that have enormous potential for economic growth in the virtual world (NFT).

The number of organizations creating "spaces" to promote corporate growth and agility will skyrocket.

Content creators, who have already found enormous success on existing social media platforms, will play a critical role in the building of this universe. The creator economy is poised to become a multibillion-dollar industry thanks to the metaverse.

The metaverse will become a marketplace for selling and trading goods, services, entertainment, and experiences, in addition to meeting and interacting. This is where companies and creators can collaborate to take advantage of the potential. It won't be enough for a creative to make a 60-second video of themselves applying a new lipstick or take images of themselves in a hotel room.

Creators will turn the metaverse into a for-profit business by:

- Commercial items, fashion, product NFTs, and IRL goods are all sold and traded.
- They can show off their NFT collections.
- We work with brands on "takeovers" and advertising.
- Virtual fashion NFTs such as trainers or clothing will be "worn" by creator avatars.
- Invite other well-known producers to create a collaborative experience for your audience.

Creators must learn to design or hire competent designers in order to make their locations more appealing to visitors. They'll be able to do this by making their own music with apps like Loudly, which use an AI-powered engine to make compositions that meet the needs and desires of artists.

Influencers will provide products and services as non-fungible tokens (NFTs), allowing their fans to share in their empire while also providing them with something of emotional worth. This is because one advantage of NFTs is that they ensure that a digital good belongs only to the buyer.

Collaboration with companies and enterprises is expected to play a significant role in this, propelling influencer marketing to new heights. This is because the metaverse will produce virtual commodities such as avatar fashion, digital space design, and much more. For the creative economy to thrive, the metaverse will open up a whole new market.

In essence, it's a win-win-win situation: if the author, community, and metaverse all work together, everyone wins. Creators can only succeed if they can reach a large enough audience and monetize their work. A platform is only used by a community if it sees value in a creator or brand. And the metaverse can only stay alive if the creators and the people who play with them stay active on the platform.

Virtual Concerts are Here to Stay

Virtual concerts held in the Metaverse are the next step in the music industry's progression. Many performers were compelled to play virtual concerts instead of real on-stage performances in 2020 due to the coronavirus.

While it may appear that this is a new trend, virtual pop artists such as Hatsune Miku have been selling out both offline and online performance venues for some years. The latent potential of virtual concerts is only now being realized by human analogues of virtual performers.

Virtual humans in the Metaverse are no longer restricted by physical restrictions. In a virtual concert, a musician can instantly change outfits or convert the stage from an outer space realm to an underwater one. The distinctions between actual and virtual reality are becoming increasingly blurred as more humans enter the Metaverse and more virtual pop stars enter our world.

Virtual concerts are held in the Metaverse, a word that refers to all online shared virtual environments. A virtual concert has the same charm as a live performance. Researchers examining virtual concerts discovered that "virtual concerts encouraged better social connection" and that the coronavirus pandemic actually aided virtual concert participants' sentiments of emotional support and empathy.

Virtual concerts can be just as entertaining and emotionally moving as real ones. While each audience member may be watching the event alone, they are all communicating with one another in the concert's shared virtual area or through live conversations.

Metaverse and gaming

In most businesses, the metaverse is still in its infancy, making it an uncertain idea for brands and investors, but not in gaming. People in the gaming industry are adopting the metaverse quickly, with Roblox and Epic Games at the front.

Epic Games' Fortnite recently hosted a virtual concert that drew ten million people. Ariana Grande was a virtual performer at the performance. Roblox Corporation, the company behind the game, has teamed up with Gucci to sell limited-edition virtual bags.

Gaming and the metaverse are inextricably linked. Many online multiplayer games, such as Minecraft, PUBG, Fortnite, and Apex Legends, function as proto-metaverses, allowing users to create digital avatars and interact with other players in real-time. In-game items such as weapon skins, wearables, and other collectibles can be purchased and traded.

AR and VR are also becoming more popular in video games, with Pokemon Go being a notable example. Overall, the metaverse adds economy to gaming by allowing players to trade valuable items and making it more immersive via AR and VR.

We may see NFT-enabled gaming becoming the norm in the future. The use of cryptocurrencies and NFTs in games is already on the rise, with more than $7 billion in NFTs transacted to date. The volume of NFTs traded will grow exponentially as the metaverse develops.

Discovering Art in the Metavesre

NFTs, which are one-of-a-kind cryptographic tokens, are used to represent digital artwork. The opportunities provided by technology to promote individual freedoms and autonomy for artists are the primary drivers in the emerging world of NFTs. Non-fungible Tokens (NFTs) are widely used digital assets in the digital world. Their value is determined by the amount of demand they create as well as their desirability. Many seasoned collectors consider themselves art fans, and they frequently develop relationships with the artists whose work they purchase. Artists from all over the world now have access to an infinite number of people who want to buy and sell art thanks to NFTs.

Digital art is also simple to do! Anyone can download Adobe Photoshop and experiment with its filters to create art that will impress them.It's also reasonably priced! Everything is within reach and inexpensive for anyone serious about curating art, from software to applications, from FL Studio to

Adobe. NFTs have enabled artists with limited resources to present their work, allowing them to create and engage in their enthusiasm for art around the world via the internet.

YUNOMETA, an NFT marketplace, connects artists, celebrities, and fans via interesting and inspiring NFTs, allowing them to create a permanent reputation and ensure that their achievements inspire future generations. The emergence of NFTs and the metaverse takes it a step further, distinguishing it and making it more accessible to a broader audience. Both artists and users benefit from the ability to create and own art in the metaverse. Mike Shinoda, Lil Pump, and a slew of other artists have jumped on the bandwagon of digitally selling their art

Contemporary artists such as XCOPY, Beeple, and others joined the new wave, using the metaverse as a platform to promote their work. In March 2021, Beeple made history when he auctioned the first-ever NFT for USD 69,346,250. For creators, the Metaverse opens up a whole new universe of possibilities for connecting with their viewers. All artists require access to the internet and some cryptocurrency in order to make their work. Renting studios and workplaces is no longer an option in the metaverse, where artists can curate their dream projects without any foundations.

While art is a kind of communication in its broadest sense, digital art provides a more efficient means of expression. YUNOMETA offers an immersive experience through their Metaverse mall. It serves as a gathering point for digital artists, businesses, and collectors. YUNOMETA has teamed up with some of the most well-known artists and companies to create a limited-edition, diversified NFT that will be available only on yunometa.com, with the purpose of making NFTs accessible to everyone on the internet.

YUNOMETA has collaborated with well-known celebrities from all around the world.

The simplicity and flexibility of digital art are key advantages. Without spending a lot of money, digital art, or NFTs, is simple to make using a limitless number of brushes, tools, and colors. Simple editing tools make it simple to make changes to digital art. Another notable advantage is the speed with which one can make digital art due to the flexibility of its workflow. For example, if you begin creating artwork late at night and are unable to complete it, you can continue working the next day, even while going to work or traveling by bus or train. These features make it easier for people to discover art in the metaverse, and they also make it easier for them to interact.

The Future of the Metaverse

It's possible that the twenty-first century may go down in history as a time when the virtual world known as Metaverse was first created and expanded. You may expect a whole new level of interactivity that goes well above what the internet has ever been able to do.

Despite the high aspirations and promises of many players in this industry, it has become clear that blockchain technology will support the metaverse and assist develop a sustainable environment for all participants. While the metaverse will have an impact on occupations and activities, it will also have a major impact on society and the way people engage with one another.

Internet and Work from Home (WFH) technological assistance were important in keeping businesses viable during COVID-19's global epidemic and allowing them to grow at a rapid pace. Post-pandemic, a number of industries, including education, have seen a dramatic shift in their use of technology.

With virtual reality (VR) wearables, the metaverse might possibly change these industries even further. Users will be able to access a different virtual world from the comfort of their own homes with the help of these devices. Interaction will be possible without long journeys, dirty air or the need to dress up for various situations. Because of the flexibility of the new curriculum, students will have the opportunity to explore a wider range of topics than is now feasible with traditional curricula.

Watching movies or having social contacts with friends after work would have virtual world alternatives without the inconveniences associated with real world activities. In other words, the Metaverse opens up a plethora of new options.

However, like with any ecosystem, the Metaverse's ability to function depends on how easy it is for individuals to do business. Various projects are already using cryptocurrencies to ease real-world and digital transactions, which is where they belong.

People will be able to move between the real world and the Metaverse more easily if fiat currency can be converted to cryptocurrencies in real time. Tokens produced by companies that facilitate virtual interactions will be used by consumers to acquire digital avatars and virtual land, as well as organize parties for loved ones, using crypto tokens.

Performing artists in the Metaverse will be compensated with cryptocurrency and able to spend their profits in the real world. It's possible that an extension of the Metaverse may lead to a fast rise in global economic activity.

With digital commodities like Non-Fungible Tokens (NFTs) resembling popular art and digital artifacts already in circulation, the Metaverse has already begun to emerge.

We can expect other companies to come around the space and this will confidently signal the new future. The Metaverse's boundaries could be blown out to infinity, allowing consumers and investors to gain access to previously unattainable wealth.

AFTERWORD

Thank you for reading this book!

In this book, you were introduced to all the different concepts you need to understand before stepping into the world of Metaverse. As a new technology, the Metaverse is still in the early stages of development. Still, its horizon is continually expanding as major firms invest in it and implement a variety of plausible use cases. We constantly hear about new metaverse ventures being created with special characteristics that set them apart from the competition. It shows what the Metaverse will look like in the future, which must be a lot better than the version we're looking at now.

Of course, the development of virtual reality, the increasing accessibility of the internet, and the widespread use of blockchain technology will all contribute to Metaverse's ability to keep up with the ever-increasing demand trends. On the other hand, we are looking forward to living in the decentralized interoperable Metaverse and making use of its many benefits. So let us prepare ourselves to be awestruck by the incredible possibilities that the Metaverse has in store for us all.

However, now that you are armed with the fundamentals of investing in Metaverse and the risks involved, it is time to get started. By now, you probably realize investing in cryptos and understanding the blockchain network isn't as intimidating as you probably thought.

Be open to learning, hone your basic understanding of Metaverse, and start investing in this market!

Good Luck,

Monika Ali Khan

Printed in Great Britain
by Amazon

80467789R00045